ADVENTURES IN FRONTIER AMERICA

Daniel Boone
and the Wilderness Road

by Catherine E. Chambers
illustrated by George Guzzi

Troll

The fire burned brightly in the great stone fireplace of the cabin. Outside the moon was high, and the stars shone.

"All right, children," said Ma. "It's time to get ready for bed."

"Oh, no—not already," said twelve-year-old John, his eyes twinkling.

"First, let Grandpa tell us a story," begged Sarah, John's younger sister.

The year was 1827. The place was a farmstead in Kentucky, where the Halliday family lived in their small log cabin.

"Well, all right," said Pa with a smile. "That is, if your ma agrees."

Ma looked up from her sewing. "I've never yet turned down a chance to hear about Grandpa's travels with Daniel Boone," she said.

Grandpa winked at her from his chair by the fire. His rugged face looked thoughtful, as he gazed up at the Kentucky rifle hanging above the mantel.

3

"So, it's Daniel Boone you young ones want to hear about. Well, I can't say I blame you," said Grandpa. "I believe he was the bravest man I ever met—a born leader, too. Why, if it wasn't for Daniel Boone, we probably wouldn't be sitting here in this fine cabin."

"Why is that, Grandpa?" asked Sarah.

Grandpa smiled. "Well, Sarah," he said, "this part of Kentucky wasn't always the way it is now, with the general store and the school and the church and farmsteads. Nope. Once it was just pure wilderness, filled with birds, buffalo, and other game. Indians came here to hunt, and maybe a few trappers passed through. But nobody lived in Kentucky, least of all settlers like us. And that's where Daniel Boone comes in. If it wasn't for him, we might never have found the way to Kentucky. He and thirty men—and

4

I'm proud to say I was one of them—carved out the Wilderness Road—the trail that leads west through the mountains into Kentucky.

"I'll never forget the day I met Boone. It was in 1756. He was a young man then—and so was I. He was tall and lean and dressed in a buckskin hunting shirt. On his head he wore a black felt hat. At his side, he carried his favorite rifle. He called it 'Tick-Licker,' and it looked something like my own Kentucky rifle that's hanging up on that wall. Although he was young, he was already well known around his home in North Carolina's Yadkin Valley as a crack shot with a rifle. But he wasn't boastful. In fact, he was just the opposite. Daniel Boone was a quiet man—and cautious, too. He always thought a bit before he said a single word.

"Well, that day, Boone was talking more than usual. He was telling a few of us farmers and hunters about a place called Kentucky. He hadn't been there himself yet—but he sure sounded like he wanted to go. He said something like, 'I hear Kentucky is the place to go if you need elbowroom. Things are likely to get a bit crowded around these parts, and Kentucky sounds like the answer. I hear there're so many wild turkeys, the sky gets dark when they all take flight. And the buffalo herds are so big, they have to be careful or the ground might sink beneath their feet. And land—why it's rich and green—just right for farming. When I get the chance, Kentucky's a place I'd like to see!'

"Daniel was just back from serving in the colonial militia as a wagon driver under the English general George Braddock. Braddock had led a troop of British and colonial soldiers across the Pennsylvania mountains in an attempt to capture Fort Duquesne from the French. At that time, both the British and the French wanted to settle in the same territory. The battle at Fort Duquesne was one of the many disputes over that land.

"Braddock's attempt failed, but at least one good thing came of it: Daniel Boone made the acquaintance of another wagon driver by the name of John Finley. Finley was a hunter who'd been to Kentucky. It was Finley who told Daniel about the great forests and bountiful game of this rich land.

"Well, I knew from the way Boone talked about Kentucky that he'd never rest till he'd found it. And I have to admit that some of that talk sparked my own curiosity. Pushing west, to find my own land and my share of adventure, started me thinking about going with Boone, if

ever he did set out for Kentucky. With a fine woodsman like Boone to lead the way, Kentucky might be a dream come true.

"I had to wait quite a few years before I got my chance to see Kentucky—and so did Daniel. Thirteen years passed. Daniel Boone was a married man with a growing family. The way I've heard it told, one day a peddler rode up to the Boone cabin. Daniel looked closely at the stranger for a minute or two, as if he were puzzled. Suddenly, he smiled as he recognized the man. It was John Finley, his old companion!

"Well, thirteen years is a long time, and the two men had a lot of talk to catch up on. And a lot of that talk was about Kentucky. Finley had been back to that land by way of a route on the Ohio River. But the river was difficult to travel, full of snags and rapids. Finley also told Boone he'd learned of another route—an old Indian trail that led west over the mountains.

"John Finley wanted to return to Kentucky, but he didn't think he was a skilled enough woodsman to find that Indian trail by himself. He asked Daniel if he'd like to go along. You can guess what Daniel said!

"That spring—I believe it was 1769—Boone, Finley, and four other men set off on a hunting expedition. Their direction was west. Their aim was to find the secret passage that led through the mountains to Kentucky. The Indians called that trail the Warriors' Path. That's because many tribes used it for war or hunting parties. But no Indians actually lived in Kentucky. All the tribes had agreed that the rich land should be a wilderness used only for hunting.

"Imagine Boone's excitement as he and the other men moved slowly through the deep forests. And imagine their

good fortune when they found the Cumberland Gap. The Cumberland Gap is a low spot in the towering mountain range. It makes a sort of natural passage through the steep mountains. Once through the mountains, the men found the Warriors' Path. They were well on their way! Well, sure enough, Kentucky turned out to be everything Finley had said it was. The men found game everywhere. And the land was beautiful. Mountains, rivers, forests, and gentle, green hills greeted the hunters as they explored this new land.

"Daniel Boone spent the next two years doing a lot more looking around in Kentucky. He hunted and trapped. He once told me he often found deer and other game by searching for 'salt licks.' Salt licks are mineral springs that contain natural salt deposits. Herds of deer and buffalo gather there to lick the earth for its salt. Boone knew the mineral springs were important because of the animals they attracted. But he also knew they might one day have another use—they just might come in handy for providing salt for future settlers. As he explored, Boone took time to mark trails for the day when he hoped to return with his family to settle in Kentucky.

"Well, I still hadn't gotten a chance to see Kentucky with my own eyes. Your Grandma Florence and I were too busy farming and raising your ma and a lot of other young ones just then. So I had to rely on Daniel Boone's reports of that new land. But my chance would come!

RICHARD HENDERSON

"In the years that followed, Boone made other trips into Kentucky. He wanted to find the perfect place for a settlement. Once, in 1773, Daniel even tried to move his own and several other families to Kentucky. They began the trip, but soon turned back after trouble with unfriendly Indians.

"Finally, in 1775, Daniel Boone's dream came true. A businessman named Richard Henderson was willing to provide Daniel with tools, horses, and supplies, if he would lead an expedition. Henderson wanted Boone to blaze a trail west into Kentucky. Then Henderson planned to claim a large piece of the land for himself and sell parts of it to other pioneers. Once the road was cleared and a settlement was built, he was sure others would follow. For his part, Boone was to receive a large tract of land.

"Daniel accepted Henderson's offer. And when I heard the famous woodsman needed volunteers, I jumped at the chance—that is, after I spoke to your grandma, of course. It seems she agreed with me that North Carolina was getting crowded. We decided we'd try our luck in Kentucky, if Daniel's expedition succeeded.

"Well, I was paid fifty-three dollars for my work on that trail—just like every one of the thirty of us who joined Daniel on his trail-blazing expedition.

"There was danger from Indians and there were hardships along the way, but I still consider that trip the best I ever made. And that's not because of those fifty-three dollars either. It's because of the freedom and the future it gave this family. Pushing west was a new chance for us, and I guess you can look around this cabin and farm to see what an adventurous spirit and hard work can build!

"When we set out, none of us knew what lay before us. Certainly none of us suspected that the poor rough trail we were blazing would be traveled by more than 200,000 settlers in the next twenty-five years. Our trail became known to settlers as the Wilderness Road.

"Boone's plan was to connect the trails that already existed into one long road that could be traveled by horses and wagons. I've got a map here—it's rough, but it shows the trail we made.

"I remember the day we set out. It was in March 1775. Everyone was in high spirits. We gathered at a fork in the Holston River, near a trail that would take us to the Cumberland Gap. Dogs barked and ran about as we readied our supplies. Soon we had loaded our packs, axes, and guns onto horses and were ready to begin our long journey.

"The sound of axes rang out, and the hard work began. Chopping away to clear and widen the trail, we passed through two valleys and continued on our way to the Cumberland Gap. It was hard, back-breaking work, and it surely sharpened a person's appetite. Luckily, we hunted a bear on our first day out and had a very good supper.

"Next, a stretch of fifty miles on the Warriors' Path lay ahead of us, waiting to be cleared of logs. At last, we turned west and followed a buffalo trail. That kind of trail is sometimes called a 'trace.' It's a path trodden smooth by herds of buffalo as they migrate year after year.

"Daniel sometimes scouted the trail ahead of us, marking the route. To measure off the miles, he would cut a large gash in a towering tree. These marks were to serve as mileposts for us and for future settlers to follow. Throughout our long journey, Daniel Boone was our leader—no doubt of it. Always cheerful and confident, his skill as a scout and woodsman kept our hearts brave and our spirits high.

"Day after day, our work continued. We chopped down trees, hauled away rocks and logs, and filled huge mud holes. Little by little, the Wilderness Road was growing.

"Next, we came to twenty miles of dead brush. We cut our way through it and found ourselves on yet another buffalo trace, thick with reeds and cane. The heavy stalks of cane, more than twenty feet high, grew in dense thickets. Slashing a trail through it, we finally came to a clearing.

We were now close to our destination on the Kentucky River.

"It had taken about ten weeks for us to reach the river. And I don't have to tell you I was not disappointed at the sight of it. All Daniel's stories about this land had been true! Boone told us of the place he'd chosen for our settlement. It was only fifteen miles away on the south bank of the river.

"As we approached the site, we spied a huge herd of buffalo grazing upon the banks of the river. The young calves pranced and jumped about. This was my first look at our future settlement.

"Despite the hard work of the past weeks, our spirits were still high. But soon we were to meet with bad fortune. As we camped one night, we were surprised by Indians. The trouble caused some men to pack up and head for home. But the rest of us were determined to stay.

"Far behind us, Richard Henderson was slowly leading a group of men and supplies carried by horses and wagons. In spite of our efforts to widen the trail, the wagons found the road too rough. The supplies had to be reloaded on the horses. The wagons were left behind.

"Henderson sent a messenger ahead to us. The letter he carried urged Boone to wait at our camp until the needed supplies could reach us.

"Although worried by our troubles with the Indians and badly in need of supplies, we couldn't help but be excited about the plentiful game and rich land of Kentucky.

"We began the work of building our settlement. A few rough cabins were built, and the beginnings of a stockade were set up. But much of our time was spent in surveying and exploring the land around us.

"Boone urged us to finish the stockade. He knew the protection it would give us was very much needed. I agreed with him, but most of the men did not. They were eager to find good land and claim it for themselves. So our fort remained only half finished.

"After much of the land around the river had been surveyed, we divided it into numbered lots. Then we drew numbers to decide fairly which lot would go to each man.

"One day in April, Richard Henderson arrived with his men, horses, and the much-needed supplies. Indeed, they were a welcome sight to us. And I dare say they were just as happy to see us.

"Our settlement had begun to grow. It was decided that we would call it Boonesborough, in honor of the man whose skill and courage had led us there.

"Henderson had brought seeds for corn and other crops. We were soon at work planting these seeds in the nearest clearings. Plans were made for a well to be dug inside the unfinished stockade. But work on both the well and the fort went slowly, for the new settlers were just as eager as we had been to survey and claim land.

"It wasn't long before we realized that the people of Boonesborough needed some rules to live by. We chose several men to lead us. Daniel Boone, his brother Squire, and a man named Richard Calloway were among them.

"There was a giant elm tree at Boonesborough. It was so big that a hundred people could sit in its shade—and that's no tall tale! Well, under that tree, we all met to discuss the laws we would need to govern Boonesborough.

"One of the most important things we talked about was a plan of Daniel's to preserve the game of Kentucky. Although the forests had been full of game when we arrived, too much wasteful hunting and trapping had already taken place. The once-plentiful herds of deer, elk, and buffalo were moving farther and farther away from us. The wisdom of Boone's plan was seen, and the bill was passed.

"Then our leaders set up a court of law. We also formed a militia to protect Boonesborough.

"Soon after our meeting, we received startling news. A messenger arrived. He excitedly told us that the colonies were now at war with England in a fight to gain independence.

"For days, we talked of little else. All of us wondered what the outcome of the war would be and how it might affect our new settlement. As for me, I favored independence.

22

"One day in June, Daniel announced that he figured Boonesborough could do without him for a short while. He planned to leave right away for North Carolina, where he had left his wife Rebecca and the rest of his family. He wanted to bring them back to Boonesborough as soon as possible.

"Indeed, I understood how Daniel felt. I often found myself thinking of your grandma and our children, waiting for the day I could bring them to their new home in Kentucky. But that day would have to wait. I wanted to be sure the cabins and fort were ready before going back to fetch the rest of the Hallidays.

"Boone set out for his old home—and his leadership was missed by the rest of us. The men had taken to bickering about the land and how it should be divided. And

24

Richard Henderson could not convince the settlers to complete the fort.

"At last, three months later, the men of Boonesborough watched excitedly as Daniel Boone led Rebecca and their children to the top of the hill that overlooked our camp. We realized that our rough outpost was about to become a true settlement. We would have to work doubly hard to make Boonesborough a home fit for women and children.

"I wonder what Rebecca Boone thought when she first spied our camp. The land was as beautiful as Daniel had promised. But the half-finished fort and cabins were surely not the prettiest sight she'd ever seen. Did she wonder why she'd left a home behind, packing up her four daughters and three sons and her few possessions? Did she wonder why she'd traveled three hundred miles to this poor camp?

"She may have. But being Rebecca, I'm sure she put all that aside. She took up her new life, full of the energy and strength that any man, woman, or child needs if they're to survive in this frontier.

"For our part, we greeted the Boones joyfully. Rebecca and the children were a welcome sight. Soon we were quite busy washing up and cutting our unruly hair and beards.

"The Boones were only the beginning of the steady stream of settlers that began to arrive in Boonesborough and the surrounding settlements. It wasn't long before our camp began to look like the beginnings of a frontier town.

"Livestock roamed about. The laughter of children playing filled the air. Everyone worked hard. There were cabins to be built. There were crops to be tended. Hunting, trapping, cooking, cleaning, and sewing were only a few of the tasks that kept us busy.

"As more families arrived, it became clear to us all that the protection of a fort was badly needed. Work to finish the fort began at last. The stockade looked like many others of that time. I'd say it enclosed an area of about seventy-five feet wide by two hundred-fifty feet long. We built all the cabins in a row, so that their back walls would form part of the long rectangle of the fort. Then work began on the large, two-story blockhouses, which were built at each corner of the fort. Between the cabins, the spaces were filled by a tall wall made of heavy wooden posts. Using knives and axes, we sharpened the tops of the posts into points. To complete our fort, we added big wooden gates at each side of the stockade. In case of attack, these gates could be securely barred.

"So, seeing at last that Kentucky was ready for us, I went back to North Carolina and brought back Florence and your ma and the rest of the Hallidays. Over the Wilderness Road we traveled, west to the land of our dreams. Through that secret passage to the frontier that Daniel Boone had found, we made our way to this very spot in Kentucky. That journey was the beginning of a new life for this family and others like us."

The fire had burned down to a bed of red embers, as Grandpa reached the end of his tale. The light cast a soft glow on the faces of the children.

Sarah smiled. "Did you and Grandma find what you were looking for in Kentucky?" she asked.

"Was it all worth it?" added John.

Grandpa thought a bit. Then he smiled and said, "It hasn't always been easy, but I'd say the good times have outnumbered the bad. And I'm proud to say we've got our freedom and plenty of the 'elbowroom' we were hoping to find at the end of the Wilderness Road. But let me ask you young ones—do *you* think it was worth it?"

"I sure do!" said Sarah.

"Why, I wouldn't trade our home for anything," said John. "We're a part of the American frontier, and that's where we belong!"

Index

*(Page numbers that appear in **boldface** type refer to illustrations.)*

This edition published in 2001.

Printed in the United States of America.

10   9   8   7   6   5   4

Cover art by Robert F. Goetzl.

Library of Congress Cataloging-in-Publication Data

Chambers, Catherine E.
    Daniel Boone and the Wilderness Road.

    (Adventures in frontier America)
    Summary: Grandpa tells his family in 1827 about
Daniel Boone's leadership in settling Kentucky.
    [1. Kentucky—Fiction.   2. Frontier and pioneer life—
Kentucky—Fiction.   3. Boone, Daniel, 1734–1820—Fiction]
I. Guzzi, George, ill.   II. Title.   III. Series: Chambers,
Catherine E. Adventures in frontier America.
PZ7.C3558Dan   1984   [Fic]   83-18291
ISBN 0-8167-0037-0 (lib. bdg.)
ISBN 0-8167-4888-8 (pbk.)